Water, Water Everywhere!

Lakes

Diyan Leake

a Capstone company — publishers for children

Raintree is an imprint of Capstone Global Library Limited, a company incorporated in England and Wales having its registered office at 7 Pilgrim Street, London, EC4V 6LB – Registered company number: 6695582

www.raintreepublishers.co.uk
myorders@raintreepublishers.co.uk

First published in hardback in 2014
Paperback edition first published in 2015

Edited by Joanna Issa and Penny West
Designed by Philippa Jenkins

Picture research by Mica Brancic
Production by Helen McCreath
Originated by Capstone Global Library Ltd
Printed and bound in China

ISBN 978 1 406 28387 7 (hardback)
18 17 16 15 14
10 9 8 7 6 5 4 3 2 1

ISBN 978 1 406 28393 8 (paperback)
19 18 17 16 15
10 9 8 7 6 5 4 3 2 1

British Library Cataloguing in Publication Data
Leake, Diyan
Lakes (Water, Water Everywhere!)
A full catalogue record for this book is available from the British Library.

Acknowledgements
We would like to thank the following for permission to reproduce photographs: Alamy pp. 6 (© Destinations by Evgeniya Moroz), 9 (© Art Directors & TRIP/Jane Sweeney), 18 (© Picture Partners), 19 (© MaximImages); Getty Images pp. 15 (Yves Marcoux), 16 (Stockbyte/altrendo images), 21 (The Image Bank/Neil Beckerman), 22a (National Geographic/Jonathan Kingston); Shutterstock pp. 4 (© Doin Oakenhelm), 5 (© Kevin Eaves), 7 (© Tatiana Grozetskaya), 10 (© feiyuezhangjie), 11, 23b (© topseller), 12 (© Marco Regalia), 13, 23c (© Eric Broder Van Dyke), 14, 23a (© Chris Geszvain), 17 (© Frank L Junior), 20 (© DNF Style), 22b (© Kevin Eaves), 22c (© WayneImage), 23a (© Chris Geszvain).

Cover photograph reproduced with permission of Alamy (© Gavin Hellier).
Back cover photograph reproduced with permission of Shutterstock/© Kevin Eaves.

We would like to thank Michael Bright and Diana Bentley for their invaluable help in the preparation of this book.

Contents

Lakes

A lake is a large body of water.

A lake has land all around it.

Some lakes have mountains around them.

Some lakes have forests
around them.

Lakes of the world

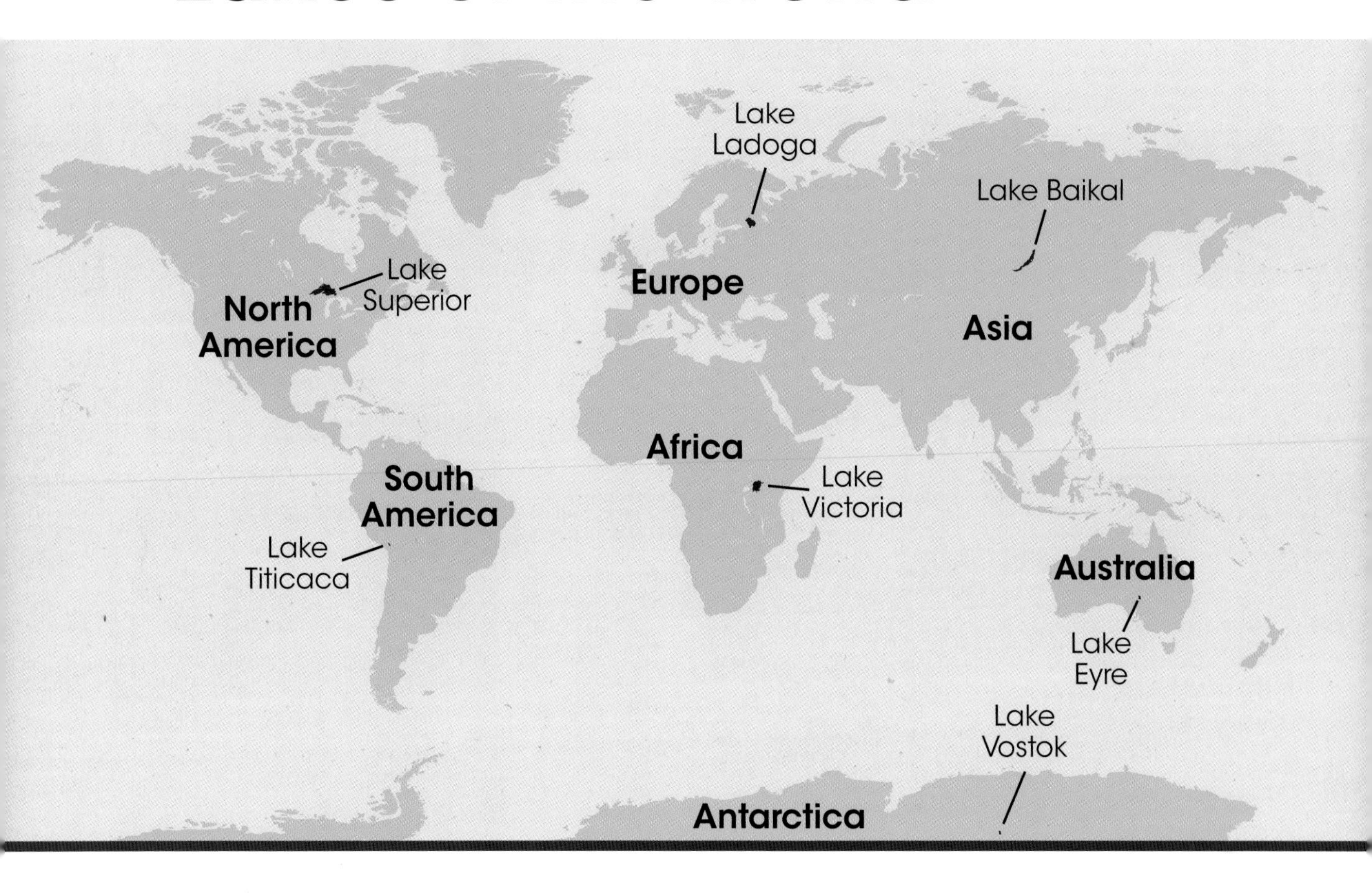

There are lakes all over the world.

Here are some of the biggest.

Lake Titicaca is one of the biggest lakes in the world.

Fresh water and salt water

Some lakes have fresh water.

This means that the water is not salty.

Some lakes have salt water.

This means that the water is salty.

What makes a lake?

People make some lakes by blocking a river with a dam.

The water in a lake may come from a river flowing into it.

How people use lakes

People enjoy being by a lake.

People can sail boats on a lake.

People need water to drink and wash.

Some of this water comes
from lakes.

Having fun on lakes

It is fun to spend time by a lake.

Stay safe! Always have an adult with you when you are near water.

Quiz

Which of these is a lake?

A

B

C

Answer on page 24

Picture glossary

dam barrier to hold back water

fresh water fresh water is not salty

salt water water that has salt in it

Index

Answer to quiz on page 22: Picture **B** shows a lake.

Note to parents and teachers

Before reading

Locate a local, UK or world lake on Google Maps. Show the children a map view that includes the lake. Can they describe what they can see on the map? Pointing to the lake, ask the children to explain what it is and what it is called. Ask the children to suggest what they might see if they were to stand on the shore of the lake. If street view is available, use it to find out what they would see.

After reading

- Arrange a visit to a local reservoir. Many reservoirs have education centres that support teaching and learning across a range of water-related themes including water conservation, water safety and the water cycle.
- Create a display backdrop showing a lake and the surrounding environment. The children could create labelled features to add to the display, such as a dam or a water treatment plant, people enjoying leisure activities, and living things on the shore and in the water.